Sports Outreach

Discovery Team

Discovery Teams are geared for groups and individuals interested in investigating the claims, challenges and teachings of Jesus Christ.

Christian Focus Publications publishes books for all ages
Our mission statement -

STAYING FAITHFUL
In dependence upon God we seek to help make his infallible word, the Bible, relevant. Our aim is to ensure that the Lord Jesus Christ is presented as the only hope to obtain forgiveness of sin, live a useful life and look forward to heaven with him.

REACHING OUT
Christ's last command requires us to reach out to our world with his gospel. We seek to help fulfil that by publishing books that point people towards Jesus and for them to develop a Christ-like maturity. We aim to equip all levels of readers for life, work, ministry and mission.

All rights reserved. No part of this publication may be reproduced, stored in a retrieval system, or transmitted, in any form, by any means, electronic, mechanical, photocopying, recording or otherwise without the prior permission of the publisher or a licence permitting restricted copying. In the U.K. such licences are issued by the Copyright Licensing Agency, 90 Tottenham Court Road, London WIP 9HE.

ISBN 1-85792-870-9

© Copyright Steve Connor 2003

Published in 2003
by
Christian Focus Publications, Ltd.
Geanies House, Fearn, Tain,
Ross-shire, IV20 ITW, Great Britain
www.christianfocus.com

Printed and bound by
J.W. Arrowsmith, Bristol

Cover Design by Alister MacInnes
Typeset in BakerSignet and AgencyFB

CONTENTS

Introduction — 5

Session 1: — 6
  What's up there?
Session 2: — 11
  God's playbook
Session 3: — 15
  Who is Jesus?
Session 4: — 21
  Who is the greatest?
Session 5: — 26
  A new coach
Session 6: — 31
  The prize
Session 7: — 35
  Power eating

Leaders' Notes — 39

Introduction to Sports Outreach Teams — 42

Memory Verses/Challenge to cut out
and keep with you. — 47

Structure form:

 **Game Plan:** Aim & desired direction of study

 **Review:** Reminder of past week's study

 **Focus:** The current session's particular verses

 **First Half:** Group/individual questions

 **Training Tips:** Thought provoking information

 **Second Half:** Group/individual questions

 **Instant Replay:** Facts and ideas to consider from the study

 **SPA:** Spiritual Profile Assessment: A quick way to measure how I am doing and where I am going spiritually. These can be done individually.

 **Action Plan:**
- **Memory Verse:** From 'focus verse'.
- **Challenge:** An application for the week.

Introduction

*'A real Christian is an odd number anyway.
He feels supreme love for someone he has never seen.
Talks familiarly with someone he cannot see.
Expects to go to heaven on the virtues of another.
Empties himself in order to be full.
Admits he is wrong in order to be declared right.
Goes down in order to go up.
Is strongest when he is weakest, richest when he is poorest,
and happiest when he feels the worst.
Dies in order to live, forsakes in order to have,
gives away so he can keep.
Sees the invisible, hears the inaudible.
Knows that which passes understanding.
No wonder people think we are crazy.'*
A W TOZER

Unfamiliar paths

What an exciting place to be, discovering for yourself the mysterious truths of the universe and the Creator that made them. Exploring is dangerous – you may find things you didn't want to know, but in the end Jesus said, 'the truth will set you free'. If you are reading this, my guess is you are involved in sport and you are checking out the Christian faith for yourself. I wish for you what Isaiah the Old Testament prophet recorded of God:

'I will lead the blind by ways they have not known, along <u>unfamiliar paths</u> I will guide them; I will turn the darkness into light before them and make the rough places smooth. These are the things I will do; I will not forsake them' **(Is. 42:16).**

Session 1: What's Up There?

Game Plan:
To explore the existence of God. To discover how this world is a system and therefore must have a system maker who reveals Himself to His creation.

Focus:
'Lift your eyes and look to the heavens: Who created all these? He who brings out the starry host one by one, and calls them each by name' **(Is. 40:26).**

'The heavens declare the glory of God; the skies proclaim the work of his hands. Day after day they pour forth speech; night after night they display knowledge. There is no speech or language where their voice is not heard. Their voice goes out into all the earth, their words to the ends of the world' **(Ps. 19:1-4).**

First Half:

1. Go around the group and ask:
    a. What is your name (relevant info... age, favourite sport,)?
    b. What is your favourite old-time TV show?
    c. Imagine that you won a game show prize and you got to pick from one of three doors? It might be a luxury trip or a total booby prize. Which door would you go for?

- Door 1 'a 3 week trip'
- Door 2 'a vehicle'
- Door 3 'a home sound/cinema system'
    If you picked door 1 what would be your worst and best case 'trip' scenario?

If you picked door 2 what would be your worst and best case 'vehicle' scenario?

If you picked door 3 what would be your worst and best case 'home/system' scenario?

However you chose, you were using a system of thought to work out the best option for you.

2. Some people say that life is merely a series of random coincidences, that there is no higher power watching over us.
   a. Has something ever happened in your life that seems more than coincidence?
   b. Example?
   c. Can someone in this group give 'testimony' to how God is working in their life?

Training Tips:
He was called 'The Columbus of The Cosmos,' Cosmonaut Yuri Gagarin was the first man in space. His epic 108 minute Earth orbital flight on 12 April 1961, was far more than just a successful operational mission. It was man's first encounter with the nether regions of space and the beginning of man's journey to the stars. On his arrival back to earth Yuri proclaimed to the world, 'God does not exist, I was in outer space and I didn't see him.' A well known minister from Texas replied, 'if he would only have taken off his space helmet he would have met him in a hurry!'

There was another reply from C. S. Lewis, the writer of the *Chronicles of Narnia* and many other helpful books, who wrote in *Christian Reflections*, 'The Russians, I am told, report that they have not found God in outer space. On the other hand, a good many people in many different times and countries claim to have found God, or been found by God, here on earth. The conclusion some want us to draw from this data is that God does not exist. But other conclusions might be drawn:'

1.We have not yet gone far enough in space. There had been ships on the Atlantic for a good time before America was discovered.

2.God does exist but is locally confined to this planet.

3.The Russians did find God in space without knowing it, because they lacked the requisite apparatus for detecting Him.

4.God does exist but is not an object either located in a particular part of space nor diffused, as we once thought 'ether' was, throughout space.

Session 1

 **Second Half:**

1. Why are we always finding our things in the last place we look?

2. Can someone define the difference between an atheist and an agnostic?

3. What is the problem with being an atheist? (See Leader's Notes – p.39)

4. Does the world have design? Is there intelligence in the world?

5. Explain Spontaneous generation... (See Leader's Notes – p.39)

Training Tips:
If there is design and if there is intelligence, reason would dictate there must be a design maker, 'higher power'. Wouldn't that design maker want to reveal itself to its creation? We find things in the last place we look because there is no reason to keep looking. The problem with being an atheist is that they make the assumption that if they have not found God therefore God does not exist. The problem with that reasoning is that they would have to have searched the entire universe and know all information. You cannot say conclusively that the keys are not in a certain room unless you have thoroughly searched the whole room.

C S Lewis started his academic life as an atheist, believing the world to be the result of random coincidence. There is no god. He realised that atheism was 'boy's theology', and became an agnostic (there is a higher power but we cannot know him). Lewis was so convinced of his agnosticism that he once wrote: 'Man cannot know God any more than Hamlet could know Shakespeare'. Lewis, a little later in his life, became a Christian. He was approached by a colleague who reminded him of his agnostic decree and asked, 'How can you be a Christian? How can you really know God?' Didn't you once write a paper defending your agnosticism?

Lewis replied, 'I was right – Hamlet could not know Shakespeare ... unless Shakespeare wrote himself into the play of Hamlet and introduced himself. God wrote himself into human history through his *creation* –'man in his image', through *nature* – Psalm 19:1 – and through his son *Jesus Christ*.'

6. Could it be that this System Maker is actually speaking but we are not in tune?

Read Focus verses again:

7. How does God communicate? Name 4 ways:
   a.

   b.

   c.

   d.

8. Would you like Him to communicate to you?

Many athletes around the world have found direction and guidance and nourishment from the Bible: calling it God's game-plan for life.

9. What is a game plan?

10. Have you ever been involved in anyone's game-plan?

Let's examine this 'manual for life' more at the <u>next team meeting</u>.

 **Instant replay:**

     God reveals Himself through His nature.
     God reveals Himself through His people.
     God reveals Himself through His Son.
     God reveals Himself through His Word.

You learned it is hard to be an atheist because you would have to search the entire universe before you realised there is no God. Ask an atheist if it is possible like Yuri Gagarin that they just didn't find God in their search, that God just might be out of their realm of knowledge.

Session 1

 SPA:

Is it new for you to be thinking in terms of listening to God, praying and reading His word? Yes/No

[ ] I've never thought in terms that God has wanted to communicate to me before.
[ ] I have not thought about God in a long time.
[ ] I have thought about God but I have been trying to avoid Him.
[ ] I have been listening and talking to God a bit and want to get to know Him more.
[ ] I have been listening and talking to God for a long time.
[ ] Other?

How important is it for you to understand and communicate with God?
Not at all [ ] A little [ ] Somewhat [ ] Quite [ ] Very [ ]

If important, how much time do you take to try to listen and communicate with God?
None [ ] Little [ ] Average [ ] Good [ ] High [ ]

 **Action Plan:**

Memory Verse:
'The heavens declare the glory of God; the skies proclaim the work of his hands. Day after day they pour forth speech; night after night they display knowledge' **(Ps. 19:1-2).**

Challenge:
This week take 'time-out' to look up into the stars and ask yourself: What must this God be like to create such vast beauty? Next, ask yourself: Does the creator of the universe want to communicate with his creation – with me?

Session 2: God's Playbook!

Game Plan:
To create a plausible argument for the Bible in a post-Christian, pluralistic society. Before we can expound Biblical truths we must seek to answer the questions about the authority of scripture and its source.

Review:
We have established that there is a system to the universe therefore there must be a system maker. That the 'System Maker' i.e. God, did create us and does communicate to us through His nature, people, Spirit and word.

Focus:
'All Scripture is God-breathed and is useful for teaching, rebuking, correcting and training in righteousness, so that the man of God may be thoroughly equipped for every good work' **(2 Tim. 3:16-17).**

First Half:

1. What is your first and second favourite sport?

2. Have you ever been flagged, carded, sent off, binned, etc?

3. Does sport need guidelines to make it fun?
   Give an example of what sport would be like without someone playing by the rules.

4. What do you think the Bible is?
   - [ ] A good paperweight?
   - [ ] A message of God's truth?
   - [ ] A bunch of old stories that we can have a good laugh at?
   - [ ] A good book to have on your shelf to impress your granny?

Session 2

Here are a few verses for sportspeople:

> *'I run in the path of your commands, for you have set my heart free...'* (**Ps. 119:32**).

> *'Therefore I do not run like a man running aimlessly; I do not fight like a man beating the air'* (**I Cor. 9:26**).

> *'So whether you eat or drink or whatever you do, do it all for the glory of God'* (**I Cor. 10:31**).

5. Can we trust the Bible? Why? Why not?

Training Tips:

'There is, I imagine, no body of literature in the world that has been exposed to the stringent analytical study that the four gospels have sustained for the past 200 years. This is not something to be regretted: it is something to be accepted with satisfaction. Scholars today who treat the gospels as credible historical documents do so in the full light of this analytical study, not by closing their minds to it.' F F Bruce, 'Foreword', in *The Historical Reliability of the Gospels*, Craig Blomberg.

Fact:
- Archaeological evidence constantly verifies places mentioned in scripture.
- Other ancient historians including Josephus, Pliny and Tacitus mention Jesus or Christianity.
- There are exceedingly more ancient biblical manuscripts than most other recognised historical figures.
- Many reliable old Bible manuscripts have been found and the content has not changed in hundreds of years. Look-up Dead Sea Scrolls for more information on the reliability of scripture.

Some more facts about the Bible:
- One thousand, six hundred years in the making,
- 40 authors and 66 books with the same theme.
- 'Theme': man is made and loved by God, man turns his back on God: – called sin. Jesus is God's solution for fallen man and man's separation from God because of his sin.
- Never once do these authors claim to write their own thoughts, over 2000 times they claim to be writing the 'words of God'.

- One sixth of the Bible is predictions of future events (prophesy), Isaiah alone made 300 predictions about Christ, 700 years before he was born! Every prediction Isaiah made came true! For example read Isaiah 52:13 – 53:12 for remarkable predictions of Christ's life. Here is a very small sample of prophecy that has been fulfilled in Christ.

> Josh McDowell wrote in *Evidence That Demands a Verdict* concerning the probability that these Prophecies came true by sheer coincidence, quoting scientist Professor Peter Stoner: 'In order to comprehend this staggering probability (the fulfillment of eight prophecies about Jesus), Stoner illustrates it by supposing that 'we take silver dollars and lay them on the face of Texas...two feet deep. Mark one silver dollar and stir the whole mass thoroughly...Blindfold a man and tell him that he that can travel as far as he wishes, but must pick up one silver dollar and say this is the right one. What chance would he have of picking the right one? The same chance that the prophets would have had of writing these prophecies and having them come true in one man' (see leader's notes).

- If a prophet of God made one wrong prophecy they were put to death. Imagine if you made one foul or one penalty and you were killed on the spot!
- It is the world's absolute bestseller, in all those years men have tried to refute the book, but it is still the most sought after book in the world.
- The evidence of the writings of scripture is much higher than any other piece of literature including the works of Caesar, Plato and Aristotle.
- Many men have lost their lives protecting the Bible.
- Many sports stars would liken the Bible as God's manual for their lives.

Second Half:

1. From 2 Timothy 3:16 we see the Bible is _____ by God.

2. Does God inspire you? How and why?

3. Have you ever been inspired by someone? How and why?

Session 2

Training Tips:
Definition: *Inspire*:
To influence, move, or guide by divine or supernatural inspiration. Biblical inspiration is God's word written by men that were inspired by God.

Paul wrote in 2 Timothy 3:16 that scripture was useful for teaching, rebuking, correcting, and training in righteousness, give an example for each sentence below, fill in the space the best you can:
- God wants to *teach* us His_____.
- God does not want us to_____ so he sometimes *rebukes* us.
- When we _____ our way, God wants to *correct* our path.
- We were made with a _____ and God wants to *train us in righteousness* so that the man of God may be thoroughly equipped for every good work.

Instant Replay:
Aren't you glad God gave us a book! Since this higher power created us and wants to communicate to us – and since His book has been so scrutinized and still found to be totally reliable don't you think we should get to know it and Him!

Action Plan:

Memory Verse:
'*All Scripture is God-breathed and is useful for teaching, rebuking, correcting and training in righteousness, so that the man of God may be thoroughly equipped for every good work*' **(2 Tim. 3:16-17)**.

Challenge:
If God designed you wouldn't He know best how you work?
Get a good version of the Bible and start reading Mark from the New Testament. Write down three ways God suggests you live and try to live them out this week:
  1.
  2.
  3.

Session 3: Who is Jesus?

Game Plan:
To examine the life and unique claims of Christ.

Review:
God does love us and wants us to know it. He speaks through nature and His people. The first part of the Bible looks ahead for that one special person who will take away sin. The second part of the Bible looks back on that special person – His life and how His followers responded to His message.

Focus:
'Thomas said to him, "Lord, we don't know where you are going, so how can we know the way?" Jesus answered, "I am the way and the truth and the life. No-one comes to the Father except through me. If you really knew me, you would know my Father as well"' **(John 14:5-7).**

First Half:

Look at the questionnaire, 'How I feel about Jesus', (SPA on p19) but don't fill it out until the end of the session.

1. What is your favourite time of day?

2. Who is your favourite active sports star?

3. What (characteristics) do you like about them?

4. Could Jesus have some of those characteristics?
Example: Who are the best three defenders in sport.... Use one sport or all sports...
I can think of several defenders that hate to let anything slip past them! Jesus is the same and hates it when someone slips away.

Session 3

Training Tips:
Here are some other examples of who Jesus was:

Born of a virgin	Matthew 1:18
Tempted	Matthew 4:1
Committed	Matthew 4:10
Compassionate	Matthew 9:36
Strong but gentle	2 Corinthians 10:1
Sinless	2 Corinthians 5:21
Humble	Phil ippians 2:6
Coach	Matthew 10:27
Intense	Matthew 21:12
Betrayed	1 Corinthians 11:23
Tough	John 19:17
Crucified	John 19:18
Rose from dead	John 20:20
Ascended to heaven	Luke 24:50-53

Training Tips:
Imagine if someone walked into the room right now and said:
'Hello, my name is _____, (who is your favourite pro athlete?)
You would quite naturally make a judgement about this supposed star's statement.

a) Either he was lying: I know what _____ is like and this poser is nothing like him!

b) Or he is mad: 'this guy is a regular nutcase, like the guy who thinks he is superman and tries to leap tall buildings in a single bound!

c) Or he is a counter-intelligence spy trying to subterfuge the _____ supporters club.

d) Or he is the real thing! ('Hey – I am one of your biggest fans – you want to go out and kick the ball around?')

C.S. Lewis wrote that Jesus was one of these three things:

a) 'A liar'. If He was a liar He certainly could not have been a good man. Good men do not lie. If He was lying what did He gain? Nothing but a brutal death.

b) 'A lunatic'. If He was a lunatic, why do psychologists, sociologists and historians say that if we followed Christ's teachings we would have world peace? Is that the sign of a lunatic?

c) 'The Lord'. He was who He claimed to be, the Son of God, the Saviour of the World. If He is real shouldn't we serve Him as our Lord?

5.   If you had never seen (pick a celebrity) _____ before you would ask him to prove it. If you weren't sure the person was the famous star he/she was claiming to be would you ask him/her to prove it?

If you don't know Jesus you would ask Him to prove it. And He did – documented several times!
- He taught with authority.
- He demonstrated His authority over nature, illness and death.
- He calmed storms (Mark 4:35-41).
- He walked on water (Matt. 14:25).
- He fed thousands with only a few loaves of bread and a few fish (Matt. 14:13-21)
- He healed blindness (John 9), paralysis (Mark 2), leprosy (Luke 17), and deafness (Mark 7).
- His healings were instantaneous. Such miracles cannot be attributed to psychosomatic healing but to one who rules over creation.
- He raised the dead (Luke 7, Matthew 9 for just a few examples)
- He rose from the dead (recorded and predicted throughout the scriptures)

Christ became the greatest influence in the world.

Someone once wrote: you can reject Him, or accept Him, but do not neglect Him.

Session 3

Training Tips:

Jesus wants you to get to know him personally. I remember being at a Fellowship of Christian Athletes summer sports camp before I was a Christian and listening to the speakers for the first time. I was struck with the fact that these high profile athletes were speaking about Jesus in the first person – as if they knew Him. I thought they were going to talk about the historical figure of Jesus but they spoke about a friend, teacher, general and saviour. I remember watching a certain TV personality. I knew about her, but I did not know her. Then one day I was speaking at a certain event and I met her. We exchanged pleasantries and asked of each other's families. I do not know her well but now I know her. At that FCA Camp the 'professionals' were speaking as if they **knew** Jesus – not just about Jesus – and that they knew Him well. 'The Lord is near to all who call on him' (Ps. 145:18). Don't depend on your feelings, but depend on the promises God has given us in His Word that He hears our prayers.

Compare:
There are several religious leaders but Jesus is the only one to claim to be God's son and only through Christ is there access to God.
- The Buddha died aged 80 in 483 BC with great respect.
- Confucius died aged 78 in 479 BC with great peace.
- Mohammed died aged 60 in 632 AD with great wealth.
- Jesus died aged 33 in great pain.

Many religions agree:
- There was a creator power source (God).
- God created rules for man to best live by; a system to live in and boundaries to observe.
- Man crossed the boundaries and broke God's rules.
- We are separated from God by this disobedience we have inherited.
- This separation disqualifies us from eternal life.

The Uniqueness of Christ:
Other world faiths had prophets who told people to do this and that to achieve a level of paradise. Jesus taught that He is God's son and that we could never in ourselves achieve anything close to earning our way to God and Heaven. Jesus again and again clearly proclaims that the only way to eternal life is trusting in Him. It's like we have this huge canyon separating us from God. It does not matter how many times we try to long jump the canyon we will never make it on our own. We just are not good enough, we can't jump that far. But there is one way – a bridge – Jesus. Jesus says, 'I am the way and the truth' John 14:6. (see illustration on p.40)

 **SPA:**

Survey: How I feel about Jesus

1. I am not sure how I feel about Jesus.
Strongly Agree [ ] Agree [ ] Neutral [ ] Disagree [ ] Strongly Disagree [ ]

2. I admire Jesus.
Strongly Agree [ ] Agree [ ] Neutral [ ] Disagree [ ] Strongly Disagree [ ]

3. I think Jesus was just a nice historical figure, no more.
Strongly Agree [ ] Agree [ ] Neutral [ ] Disagree [ ] Strongly Disagree [ ]

4. I think Jesus was a crazy man who misled many people.
Strongly Agree [ ] Agree [ ] Neutral [ ] Disagree [ ] Strongly Disagree [ ]

5. I like Jesus but I don't know Him very well.
Strongly Agree [ ] Agree [ ] Neutral [ ] Disagree [ ] Strongly Disagree [ ]

6. Jesus scares me.
Strongly Agree [ ] Agree [ ] Neutral [ ] Disagree [ ] Strongly Disagree [ ]

7. I don't think Jesus really understands me and my life.
Strongly Agree [ ] Agree [ ] Neutral [ ] Disagree [ ] Strongly Disagree [ ]

8. I know that Jesus loves me.
Strongly Agree [ ] Agree [ ] Neutral [ ] Disagree [ ] Strongly Disagree [ ]

9. I know that Jesus is the son of God and was raised from the dead.
Strongly Agree [ ] Agree [ ] Neutral [ ] Disagree [ ] Strongly Disagree [ ]

10. I know that Jesus made an awesome and unthinkable sacrifice for me and I want to serve Him and His Father the rest of my life.
Strongly Agree [ ] Agree [ ] Neutral [ ] Disagree [ ] Strongly Disagree [ ]

11. I want to learn more about serving Jesus and following Him.
Strongly Agree [ ] Agree [ ] Neutral [ ] Disagree [ ] Strongly Disagree [ ]

Session 3

 Action Plan:

Memory Verse:
'I am the way and the truth and the life. No one comes to the Father except through me' **(John 14:6).**

Challenge:
- Do you know for certain that if you died today you would go to heaven?
- If you were standing before God and He said why should I let you in what would you say?

The only correct answer is, 'because I trust that Your son died for my sins and took my sin away. I trust (have faith) in your son.'

If someone asked you if you were married you would know! Yes or no?
If someone asked you if you were a Christian would you know? Yes or no?

Can you say yes?

Session 4: Who is the greatest?

Game Plan:
The purpose of this group meeting is to explore the Biblical concept of sin.

Review:
Jesus' uniqueness lies in the fact that He is the Son of God and His death on the cross takes away sin for all those that trust in Him.

Focus:
'For the wages of sin is death, but the gift of God is eternal life in Christ Jesus our Lord' (Rom. 6:23).

First Half:

Since the end of the last century there have been a number of lists of the greatest sports stars ever.

1. Who are your greatest?
    Choose three sports:
    a.
    b.
    c.

2. Who was the greatest of the three?

3. How would you rate them on a scale from 1 – 10?

4. Of the three sports who is the greatest 'active' sports star?
    Rate them on a scale 1 – 10:

    1 - 2 - 3 - 4 - 5 - 6 - 7 - 8 - 9 - 10

Session 4

Who is the all round best person you know?
Rate them on a scale 1 – 10:

1 - 2 - 3 - 4 - 5 - 6 - 7 - 8 - 9 - 10

Who is your best living person in the world? Doesn't have to be in sport.
Rate them on a scale 1 – 10:

1 - 2 - 3 - 4 - 5 - 6 - 7 - 8 - 9 - 10

Now (privately) where do you rate yourself?

1 - 2 - 3 - 4 - 5 - 6 - 7 - 8 - 9 - 10

Second Half:

1. Have you ever met someone who has never sinned?

 **Training Tip:**

'For all have sinned and fall short of the glory of God' **(Rom. 3:23).**

'For the wages of sin is death, but the gift of God is eternal life in Christ Jesus our Lord' **(Rom. 6:23).**

Someone once wrote sin is a disease.
'We are not sinners because we sin, we sin because we are sinners.'

Sin is an ancient bow and arrow term originally meant for missing the bull's eye. We were created for a purpose but because of our sinful nature (like a disease) we do not completely measure up to perfection. We can't hit the bull's eye! Sin is not just doing wrong things; it is also an attitude of rejecting or ignoring God and His plan for our life. Sin separates us from God.

It is a bad deal! I was born with the disease and so were you! From the beginning Adam and Eve had it made, paradise! All God required from them was one thing.

2. What was the one thing God required of them?

'And the LORD God commanded the man, "You are free to eat from any tree in the garden; but you must not eat from the tree of the knowledge of good and evil, for when you eat of it you will surely die"' **(Gen. 2:16-17).**

3. Then how can we bridge the separation that sin creates between man and God?

The bad news is: We never will.
It's like trying to long jump to heaven on our own power, it doesn't matter how hard we try, we will not make it: (see the diagram on page 41)

4. What is the penalty for sin? 'For the wages of sin is death…
    - Separation from God.
    - This separation from God has been described as a horrible torment.
    - Some have argued exactly how bad it will be but nobody who has studied the Bible recommends hell as a place of residence!

'Do not be deceived: God cannot be mocked. A man reaps what he sows. The one who sows to please his sinful nature, from that nature will reap destruction; the one who sows to please the Spirit, from the Spirit will reap eternal life' **(Gal. 6:7-8).**

This means that all our activity: what we do, what we say, and what we desire will always affect us.

5. If God loves us how could He let sin happen?

   - God did not want the world and His creation to suffer, but He wanted His creation to have the freedom to love. Sadly we abused that freedom by rebelling from Him.
   - We were given boundaries and our ancestors broke those boundaries and we inherited this 'separation from God.'
   - Even if we try really hard we do not measure up to what God wants in us.
   - Really look at yourself – are you good enough to stand in front of the all mighty God?
     'For all have sinned and fall short of the glory of God' **(Rom. 3:23).**

The good news is: We don't have to make it to heaven on our own! *'...the gift of God is eternal life...'* **(Rom. 6:23)**.

- We can't and never will bridge the gap between man and God. We get a *free* pass!
- Isn't it cool that eternal life is what everyone in the world really wants: paradise, heaven, life forever... and it is free! Why is it free? Because we could not afford to buy it! We really don't have much to offer!

Okay then if it is free: How do we get it? *'...In Christ Jesus our Lord'* **(Rom. 6:23)**.

- Christ bridges the gap between man and God.
- How does Jesus bridge that gap?

'For God so loved the world that he gave his one and only Son, that whoever believes in him shall not perish but have eternal life. For God did not send his Son into the world to condemn the world, but to save the world through him. Whoever believes in him is not condemned, but whoever does not believe stands condemned already because he has not believed in the name of God's one and only Son' **John 3:16-18)**.

Have you trusted Jesus to take away your sin?
That is why we need Jesus Christ. Jesus was without sin – When Christ died on the cross, all our sins were transferred to Him, and He took the punishment we deserve. Now, when we give our lives to Him, He cleanses us of all our sins and completely takes them away. And that's why I can face death without fear — because in Christ all my sins have been taken away, and I don't need to fear God's judgment.

Would you like Him to?
By a simple act of faith, ask Christ to come into your life and take away your sins — and He will. Then begin every day by thanking God that *'since we have been justified through faith, we have peace with God through our Lord Jesus Christ'* **(Rom. 5:1)**.

Here is a suggested prayer:

'Then I acknowledged my sin to you and did not cover up my iniquity. I said, "I will confess my transgressions to the LORD" — *and you forgave the guilt of my sin'* **(Ps. 32:5)**.

I know I am not worthy to be called a child of yours. I do not deserve your gift of eternal life. I need your forgiveness. Thank you for sending your Son to die for me to pay my sinful debt that I may be forgiven. Thank you that you raised Jesus to give me new life. Please forgive me and change me that I may live with Jesus as my Lord and Saviour. Amen'

Instant Replay:
In fact the whole world has inherited the disease (sin) but the good deal is: we can also inherit the cure for sin – Jesus!

What is the cure for sin?
'For just as through the disobedience of the one man the many were made sinners, so also through the obedience of the one man the many will be made righteous' **(Rom. 5:19).**

Action Plan:

Memory Verse:
'For the wages of sin is death, but the gift of God is eternal life in Christ Jesus our Lord' **(Rom. 6:23).**

Challenge:
Have you ever been given a gift? Well this week think about the most awesome gift you can ever and will ever receive. Eternal life from Jesus Christ. Happy Birthday and Merry Christmas all rolled into one – Big Time!

Session 5: A New Coach

Game Plan:
To investigate the work of God's Holy Spirit and have a clearer understanding of God's Lordship over us.

Review:
We have seen that we can't make it on our own because of the sin that is in us; but Christ died for us as a sacrifice. We can accept or reject that gift of eternal life. But we can't earn it on our own.

Focus:
'But you will receive power when the Holy Spirit comes on you; and you will be my witnesses in Jerusalem, and in all Judea and Samaria, and to the ends of the earth' **(Acts 1:8).**

First Half:

1. If you could make the biggest sporting play of the year what would it be?
   a) Passing _____ to win the Grand Prix championship?
   b) Scoring winning goal in a_____ Cup Final?
   c) Beating_____ at Wimbledon?
   d) Scoring for _____ in the last minute of a game against _____?
   e) Others?

2. If you won a prize to spend time with your favourite sports or movie star, who would it be with?

3. What car would you pick them up in?

4. Where would you eat?

5. Where in the world would you take them to?

Fill out: Influence Survey.

Rate the following according to the degree of influence they have on your thinking and behaviour. Check the category that best applies:

Influence	None	A Little	A Lot	An Awful Lot
Mom				
Dad				
Team Mates				
Church Friends				
Television Shows				
Advertisements				
Films				
Radio				
Family Members				
Books				
Magazines				
Teachers				
Bosses				
Coaches				
Weather				
Christian Leaders				
Sports Heroes				

Second Half:

I. As a Christian should Jesus influence your life –

   a) Never! I want nothing to do with Him [ ]

   b) Only on Sundays and major holidays [ ]

   c) He's too busy. He really isn't interested in me [ ]

   d) He should influence me totally [ ]

Session 5

 Training Tips:
So if Jesus died and went to be with His father how can He have an influence on me?

Let's look at what Jesus says about the influence God will have on us through the Holy Spirit!

> 'But when he, the Spirit of truth, comes, he will guide you into all truth. He will not speak on his own; he will speak only what he hears, and he will tell you what is yet to come. He will bring glory to me by taking from what is mine and making it known to you. All that belongs to the Father is mine. That is why I said the Spirit will take from what is mine and make it known to you' **(John 16:13-15).**

When Jesus was crucified, the curtain in the Temple in Jerusalem was torn. God had a special presence in the Temple, in a room called the 'Holy of Holies'. The curtain dividing the room was torn from top to bottom to signify that God was to fulfill His promise and change His residency. His new home is in the hearts of believers when we invite the third person of the Trinity, the Holy Spirit to reside in the very core of our existence. Christ's death provides the antidote for sin. When we invite Christ into our lives we join a special team and receive a king's inheritance (we were bought with a king's ransom). But with the new inheritance, come new responsibilities.

Jesus promised his fearful lonely disciples that He would be with them 'Always until the very end of the age'. There is a very practical reason for God being present in us in the form of the Holy Spirit. If Jesus decided to stay in bodily form as one man you would not get close to him. Imagine lining up to see Jesus. Perhaps because he is so busy you could only see him for one minute. The disciples spent three years with Jesus and they still blew it, but you are happy to see him for a brief sixty seconds. You wait for your turn; unfortunately, there are six billion people on the planet and they all, for one reason or another, want to meet him. Remember Jesus does not care about rank or how clever you are, he wants to see you too! You get in line and wait and wait and wait. Unfortunately, you really need to use the facilities, so you get out of line and dash to the toilet. A big angel on crowd-control sees you return to the line, mistakes you as a queuejumper, and throws you to the end of the line. What a bad deal, you are the last person in the world that gets to see Jesus! Add it up! Add up six billion, times one minute! You are going to have to wait 11,500 years just to see Jesus for one minute! That is a lot of waiting around!

Fortunately, we can breath easy; he is here with you now as you read this book. He promises to never leave you and he will never forsake you. We do not have to wait around merely to get a glimpse of the super star; the super star wants to have an intimate friendship with you. You have access to God through a gift God gives you in the form of the third person of the Trinity – the Holy Spirit. He is with you now – you never need to walk alone. (Taken from *A Sporting Guide for Eternity*)

2. Does God want you to be under his management?

Whenever a player is transferred they have to make changes. I remember switching teams: it was a hard adjustment. I liked my old coach and his philosophy of play. It was not easy learning the new plays and new skill techniques. My attitude at first was a little defiant and I reverted to my old coaching habits sometimes. This infuriated the new coach and he suggested that: ' If you want to play for me and this team, you better play my way'. He was the coach and I was under new management. It was really a matter of choosing whether I really wanted to be on this particular team. I really wanted to play for him and slowly I learned new techniques and improved. Other guys were more stubborn and didn't stay.

God wants to be our coach and gives us help:

Read:
'But the fruit of the Spirit is love, joy, peace, patience, kindness, goodness, faithfulness, gentleness and self-control. Against such things there is no law. Those who belong to Christ Jesus have crucified the sinful nature with its passions and desires. Since we live by the Spirit, let us keep in step with the Spirit' **(Gal. 5:22-23).**

The Holy Spirit's central ministry to us is to:
- Enlighten us (Eph. 1:17-18).
- Make us new (John 3:5-8).
- Make us good (Rom. 8:14).
- Give us assurance (Rom. 8:16).
- Equip us with tools for ministry (1 Cor. 12:4-11).

3. Does God want to influence your life?

4. Have you asked the Holy Spirit into your life to fill you and make you more like Christ?

Session 5

 **Instant Replay:**
Jesus did not leave us alone but gave us the Holy Spirit.
God influences, inspires and changes you through the Holy Spirit?
How does God want you to be more like Him in your sport?
How does God want you to be like Him in the rest of your life?

 Action Plan:

Memory Verse:
'But you will receive power when the Holy Spirit comes on you' **(Acts 1:8).**

Challenge:
Ask God to fill you with power. Ask God to fill you with His Spirit. Fire your old coach (self) and make Christ the centre of your life.

Session 6: The Prize

Game Plan:
The objective of this team meeting is to become aware that earthly rewards do not fully satisfy. Paul wants us to train and compete for a 'prize' that will 'last for ever' – total satisfaction.

Review:
To be filled with the Holy Spirit, then, is to be so inspired by, guided by, and changed by Him that we will reflect God's moral character and be strengthened by His power.

A few traits we will reflect when we are filled by His Spirit. We will be: 'loving, joyful, peaceful, patient, kind, good, faithful, gentle, self-controlled' **(Gal. 5:22, 23)**.

Focus:
'Do you not know that in a race all the runners run, but only one gets the prize? Run in such a way as to get the prize. Everyone who competes in the games goes into strict training. They do it to get a crown that will not last; but we do it to get a crown that will last forever. Therefore I do not run like a man running aimlessly; I do not fight like a man beating the air. No, I beat my body and make it my slave so that after I have preached to others, I myself will not be disqualified for the prize' **(I Cor. 9:24-27)**.

First Half:

1. What is the best place in your area to get Indian food?

2. If that restaurant was to win a prize would it be for a) wicked service, b) wicked value, c) wicked breath, d) wicked flavour, e) wicked after effects?

3. Have you ever won a prize? What was it?

4. If you could win any award or achievement, what would it be?

5. Do we ever spend too much time chasing prizes that don't count?

6. List ten goals, dreams, awards or prizes you would like to achieve.

 **Second Half:**

Reread Focus verse.

1. What kind of a prize was Paul talking about?

2. How can we win that prize?

3. Ask yourself if you would like to have the prize of eternal life?

Training Tip:
San Francisco 1957. A tall, skinny 10 year-old schemed how to sneak inside Kaiser Stadium. All year he had waited for the big (American Football) game between the 49ers and the Cleveland Browns. It represented his one chance to see his idol, Jim Brown, the greatest American footballer of the day.

The boy slipped into the stadium late into the match. He knew it would not be easy but it would be worth it to see his hero in real life. Ghetto life had taken its toll on the boy, malnutrition had ravaged his legs so that he needed metal splints to get around.

Even so, he made it into the stadium and waited patiently in the players tunnel. Finally the match was over and the boy struggled to stand tall, waiting for his hero. Brown came round the corner and graciously signed the autograph before turning for the locker room.

Before Brown could get away, the boy tugged his jersey and confessed: 'Mr Brown, you are my idol. I have your picture on my wall and though my family cannot afford a television, I watch you when I can'.

Brown put his hand on the boy's shoulder and thanked him before heading for the locker room. But the boy reached up and tugged Brown's jersey again. Brown turned and looked at the boy's big brown eyes and asked impatiently 'Yes?'

The boy cleared his throat and said matter-of-factly, 'Mr Brown, one day I am going to break every one of your records.'

'What is your name, son?'

'Orental James Simpson, sir' said the boy 'but my friends call me OJ'. OJ Simpson went on to break all but one of Jim Brown's records, but sadly through the murder trial that came up (whether innocent or guilty) years later all of Simpson's records meant nothing. (Taken from *Cross Training Manual* by Gordon Thiessen)

Records and achievements are great, we love awards but they do not last. Jesus wants us to set our sights on the prize that will last for eternity.

Training Tip:
In our focus verse the Apostle Paul wrote that we could receive a 'Crown', that crown signifies a new life. We are adopted into royalty. With this adoption we receive an inheritance! Matthew 25:34 'Then the King will say to those on his right, 'Come, you who are blessed by my Father; take your inheritance, the kingdom prepared for you since the creation of the world?'

4. What will we inherit? (See Leader's Notes – p.39)
   -
   -
   -
   -

Instant Replay:
Answer this question to yourself before we close in prayer: do you want to have the prize that lasts forever, eternal life with God?

Close in a brief prayer:
'Father, thank you that you sent your Son to die for us that we may have your eternal prize. Forgive me for I realise that I am not worthy of the prize. Help me to live my life for you, Amen.'

Session 6

 SPA:
Look at the Stadium illustration and ask yourself where you want to be in light of this awesome inheritance?

 Action Plan:

Memory Verse:
'Everyone who competes in the games goes into strict training. They do it to get a crown that will not last; but we do it to get a crown that will last forever' **(I Cor. 9:25).**

Challenge:
Remember all that trust in Christ for salvation get a crown and an inheritance. It is like becoming a trillionaire and much more. We should be the happiest people on earth! It makes any other prize pale into insignificance! *'Come, let us sing for joy to the LORD; let us shout aloud to the Rock of our salvation'* **(Ps. 95:1).**

Session 7: Power Eating

Game Plan:
To encourage the Discovery Team to appreciate the necessity of spiritual nourishment.

Review:
When we realise what we get out of the Christian deal we should really be pumped-up! Joyful in all circumstances! *'Be joyful always; pray continually; give thanks in all circumstances, for this is God's will for you in Christ Jesus'* **(I Thess. 5:16-18)**.

Focus:
'Your words are what sustains me; they are food for my hungry soul' (Jer. 15:16).

First Half:

1. If you have a big group: Write out the following answers to the five statements below on a slip of paper. Put the statements into a hat and have some one draw them out and read the answers. Have the group try to guess who the slip of paper belongs to.

If I had to describe myself as a:
a) Kind of dog, it would be a_____.
b) Automobile, (model and colour), it would be a_____.
c) Kind of music, it would be_____.
d) Animal in the zoo, it would be_____.
e) TV or cinema actor, it would be_____.
f) Type of food, it would be _____.

2. What is your favourite food?

3. How many calories should a high performance athlete take in from:
Carbohydrates (Breads, pastas)? (%) 10 [ ] 15 [ ] 20 [ ]40 [ ] 60 [ ]80 [ ]100 [ ]
Proteins (meats, nuts)? (%) 10 [ ] 15 [ ] 20 [ ]40 [ ] 60 [ ]80 [ ]100 [ ]
Fats (stuff that tastes good!) (%) 10 [ ] 15 [ ] 20 [ ]40 [ ] 60 [ ]80 [ ]100 [ ]

4. How much will eating properly enhance your performance?
(%) 10 [ ] 15 [ ] 20 [ ]40 [ ] 60 [ ]80 [ ]100 [ ]

 **Training Tips:**
Do you eat and drink the right types of food to fuel your training and performances? Nutrients help you recover from tough training sessions and prepare you for competitions. Young athletes also have to take in consideration that their body is growing.

We take in mental nutrients as well. Training our bodies is only part of the job but being mentally prepared, the right frame of mind, is as, if not more important for competition. Attitude, staying motivated, setting goals, staying and keeping focused and controlling anxiety are all part of sport.

5. What kind of food feeds our minds?

 **Second Half:**

1. What are some ways we take in spiritual nourishment?

2. Have you skipped a meal recently? Who has gone the longest on this team without eating?

3. What would it be like if you had to run a marathon after not eating for three days?
'Do not conform any longer to the pattern of this world, but be transformed by the renewing of your mind. Then you will be able to test and approve what Gods will is, his good pleasing and perfect will' **(Rom. 12:2).**

We are renewable people; we continually renew our supply of oxygen. We continually renew our supply of sleep and our caloric intake.

4. As Christians do we need to be spiritually renewed?

5. Give some examples of spiritual renewal?
-
-
-

Bible study is a big part of being a strong Christian. Jesus said in John 8:31 *'If you hold to my teaching (my word) you are really my disciples.'*

The psalmist wrote, *'I have hidden your word in my heart so that I do not sin against YOU'* **(Ps. 119:11).**

6. Is there a right and wrong time to study God's word?

Training Tips:
We will hit these issues hard in the Impact Team series. But for now let me encourage you that you will get spiritual nourishment through:
- Prayer
- Encouragement (fellowship)
- Scripture reading.
- Sharing your faith.

Where should I start reading my Bible?

There are many great modern versions of the Bible on the market. They have not changed the accuracy of God's word, just made it a bit clearer to understand. If you are new to scripture reading I suggest reading the Gospel of John. Then go to Acts and Galatians. Get a devotional to bring you to places in the scripture that you are not familiar with. Find a church ('faith community') that is committed to encouraging your spiritual growth. Start talking to God (prayer). If you can communicate, you can pray. It is that simple.

Here are 4 questions you could consider to help you study the Bible.
- What does it say?
- What does it say about God?
- What does that mean for me?
- How do I respond?

Session 7

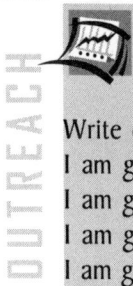

SPA:
A goal not written down is merely a wish:

Write down four spiritual goals:
I am going to read_____ this week
I am going to pray for_____ this week
I am going to go to this_____ Christian meeting.
I am going to talk to this _____ Team mate about my faith this week.

Instant Replay:
Just as I need nourishment: to eat, rest and be mentally prepped for competition, I need spiritual nourishment – Scripture, time with God, time with like-minded Christians, time to tell others about how awesome Christ is.

Action Plan:

Memory Verse:
'Your words are what sustains me; they are food for my hungry soul' **(Jer. 15:16).**

Challenge:
Just as I carve out time in my day to prepare for my sport, I will carve out time to get spiritually prepped; food for my hungry soul!
Today I will read:_____

LEADER'S NOTES:

Session 1
<u>Atheist:</u> one who denies the existence of God. How can you prove that God doesn't exist?
<u>Agnostic:</u> : a person who holds the view that any ultimate reality (such as God) is unknown and probably unknowable; *broadly* : one who is not committed to believing in either the existence or the nonexistence of God or a god.

Design Maker
The teleological argument for the existence of God is the argument from design. That is, the universe appears to have been designed, therefore there must have been a designer. One of the most famous teleological arguments came from William Paley. He offered the 'Watchmaker' illustration. If you found a watch in an empty field, you would rightly conclude that there was a maker of that watch because of its obvious design. Therefore, when you look at the even more complex world that we live in, we must imply that there was a maker of the world.

<u>Spontaneous Generation:</u> The propagation of living organism without apparent cause. Something starting from nothing or non-living matter.

Session 2
Evidence that Demands a Verdict, Josh McDowell (Thomas Nelson, ISBN 0840743785). See also *The Authority of the Bible,* Colin Peckham (Christian Focus, ISBN 1 85792 436 3).

Session 6
What will we inherit? (A few examples)
- **Salvation:** 'The LORD is my strength and my song; he has become my salvation' (Ex. 15:2).
- **Freedom:** It is for freedom that Christ has set us free. Stand firm, then, and do not let yourselves be burdened again by a yoke of slavery' (Gal. 5:6).
- **New & eternal life:** 'In his great mercy he has given us new birth into a living hope through the resurrection of Jesus Christ from the dead, and into an inheritance that can never perish, spoil or fade—kept in heaven for you' (1 Pet. 1:3).
- **Ministering Angels:** 'Are not all angels ministering spirits sent to serve those who will inherit salvation?' (Heb. 1:14).
- **Become a new creation:** 'Therefore, if anyone is in Christ, he is a new creation; the old has gone, the new has come!' (2 Cor. 5:17).
- **A new home:** 'In my Father's house are many rooms; if it were not so, I would have told you. I am going there to prepare a place for you' (John 14:2).
- **Purpose:** 'For we are his workmanship, created in Christ Jesus unto good works, which God hath before ordained that we should walk in them' (Eph. 2:10).

Leader's Notes

So where am I at spiritually with the Lord? Am I on God's team?

[ ]   I am so lost I did not even know there was a game being played.

[ ]   I know there is a game going on but I just can't find the stadium.

[ ]   I found the stadium but I am on the outside.

[ ]   I am watching God's team from far away.

[ ]   I am watching God's team up close.

[ ]   I want to be on God's team but am not sure how to join.

[ ]   I am new on God's team, learning a lot, and enjoying being part of it.

[ ]   I am on God's team but I am not making any impact.

[ ]   I am on God's team and playing as hard as I can!

[ ]   I am on God's team but I keep fouling!

Leader's Notes | 41 |

SPORTS OUTREACH

'For the wages of sin is death' (separation from God)...

'The free gift of God is eternal life through Christ' **(Rom. 6:23).**

Introduction to Sports Outreach Teams (Small Groups)

The Sports Outreach Team meeting is the heart of the whole ministry concept. A 'Sports Outreach Team' is like a 'huddle': an American football term whereby a team gathers together on the pitch in a small circle and discusses various plays and strategy. A Sports Outreach Team meeting is a small group committed to investigate the scriptures in the context of their sport and life:

We have a series of three team meetings:

Sports Outreach: Discovery Teams
Sports Outreach: Impact Teams
Sports Outreach: Leadership Teams

- **Discovery Teams** are geared for groups and individuals intersted in investigating the claims, challenges and teachings of Christ.
- **Impact Teams** aim to challenge and develop the believer into a stronger walk in Christ.
- **Leadership Teams** seek to challenge and train Christians to be active and fully committed followers of Christ: able to reproduce reproducers and lead Discovery and Impact Teams.

Research suggests that most people from unchurched backgrounds attribute their conversion to Christianity by the influence of a Christian friend – relationships. Sport provides an excellent way of making friends and building relationships, these can be developed into evangelistic opportunities.

Small group meetings link the 'Big Events' and Camps into a series of consistent opportunities for proclaiming God's word and encouraging spiritual growth. Many of us have been to outreach functions where we have seen youth and adults indicate that they have trusted Christ as Lord and Savior. What an exciting time to see those for whom we have been praying apparently open up their hearts to Christ.

However, joy can turn to disappointment as we realize that not all the youth that have made a profession of faith are growing in their relationship to Christ. Why do some seem to wilt on the vine? Possibly many causes, but all too often the problem is lack of carry-on or follow-up from more mature Christians.

The church is seeing the value in having a ministry to the sports world. 'It's a knock-out', five-a-side's, and pool parties have been part of the arsenal of every youth group for years. But what comes next? Often a young person whose whole life revolves around sport will be discontent with the youth group or club geared to music or drama. Sports OutreachTeams focus on presenting Christ's salvation and His Lordship in a way that interests people in the world of sport.

The Hows, Whens, Wheres and Whos

How often should we meet?
The answer to this question varies. Some group leaders will want to meet every week while others will meet once or twice a month. Whatever you do, plan the meetings well and be consistent.

When do Sports Outreach Teams meet?
Again the answer is varied. Whether you meet after church, during club time, lunch, evenings, after school, before training or after training, early mornings before work, or Saturdays after a round of golf. Survey your group and choose the best possible time.

Where should we meet?
Many Christian groups are successful because they meet at their local church or school property in a central location. Still others like having a place that is away from church or school, the atmosphere can be less formal. Each group will have to survey their area to see which kind of setting will best accomplish their goals – to lead athletes to Christ and help them to mature in their faith. Our best model of small groups in the United Kingdom has been the Alpha Course and Christianity Explored. Many of their meetings are at night and centred around a meal.

Who leads the Team?
Sports Impact leaders need three criteria: to love Jesus; to love people and to love sport, and in that order! Obviously by now if you have read this far into the book you are interested in developing a sports ministry. From experience we want to encourage you to get help and prayer support. Leaders should take care not to dominate the meetings but rather, to facilitate discussion. But leadership is important for consistency and to maintain order.

In the book of Titus we find the young man Titus was left on the island of Crete to organize the Cretan Christians into churches. Over and over Paul tells Titus to encourage the Cretans 'do what is good'.

'*Similarly, encourage the young men to be self-controlled. In everything set them a good example by doing what is good. In your teaching show integrity, seriousness and soundness of speech that cannot be condemned, so that those who oppose you may be ashamed because they have nothing bad to say about us*' **(Titus 2:6-8).**

Tips for leading Sports Outreach Teams

- Start and finish with a prayer. Encourage the young people to pray silently or aloud if they want to.

- Think of an interesting icebreaker, story or topic of conversation to open with – about their day/the talk/sport etc.

- Have the Bible open and encourage the group to read it aloud and/or in turn.

- Present the questions in different ways, re-phrase where necessary and make them relevant/topical, maybe with a sporting example.

- Let the group give their own responses to the question, don't talk too much or always be giving them the answer. Keep it Bible-based and Christ-centred.

- Keep it short and sweet – don't be boring! If you don't enjoy it, the group probably won't either!

- Be honest and don't compromise on the truth.

- Don't make it too formal; you are their friend as much as their coach.

- Don't disappear at the end. Chat about other things, they may want to ask questions.

- Make sure you have prepared beforehand by looking at the passage, thinking of questions and praying.

- Do not preach: Our aim is to get alongside athletes and help point them to the cross.

- Jesus was a master of teaching through questions and stories.
    - These studies are meant to be deductive and inductive.
    - It is not always necessary to use sporty anecdotes; eventually you may run out of sports stories and metaphors. Feel free to bring in other stories but remember athletes have unique goals, stresses and time demands.

- Easily answered questions should be used to start with.

  - 'What's your favourite old time TV show?' usually gets a good laugh. This will enable the group to feel more confident to participate in the deeper questions.

  - It is a general rule that the 'first half' questions are designed to encourage discussion; the 'second half' of the team meeting is created to introduce biblical themes. But it will rarely go that way.

  - All answers are fine, but if the answers are getting too off track, the leader should feel free to answer 'That is interesting; let's talk about that later.' Then move back towards the aims of the meeting.

  - The discussion should not be allowed to go off at too many tangents. Satan loves to throw in 'smoke screens' when the topic is relevant to people's needs.

- It is good to sit in a circle especially if it is a small group.
  - Any who want to sit/stand at the back should be gently encouraged to join in the group.

- Questions will eventually arise which you may not be able to answer.
- It is best not to try to bluff a way through.
- It is better to simply admit you do not know the answer and promise to get back with them at the next meeting.

- A member of the group can be encouraged to do the reading, but it should not be sprung on someone who may be embarrassed. 'How do you pronounce Abimalech?'

- Prayer should be introduced to the group slowly. A leader simply praying 'Thank you God for friends and sport, amen,' may speak much more to seekers than a long theological prayer.

- If a question is asked and there is no immediate response the leader should feel free to wait, allow a bit of time and then possibly restate the question.
  - Silence can be beneficial if it is not too long.

- The leader should never criticize or make anyone feel foolish about his or her answer to a question.
  - The leader should allow others to contribute answers to people's questions. Many times the young people's answers will be better than the leaders!

Leader's Notes

'Many of *the Samaritans from that town believed in Jesus because of the woman's testimony...*' **(John 4:39).**

We can see from the example of the Samaritan woman in John's gospel how effective testimony can be.

Whether you are a Coach or Huddle Leader, you will probably have an opportunity to speak personally about your faith and how you became a Christian.

'Always be prepared *to give an answer to* everyone *who asks you to give* the reason *for* the hope *that you have. But do this with gentleness* and respect' **(1 Pet. 3:15).**

Looking at the Bible:

Here are 3 questions you could consider to help you as you prepare any Bible study:
- What does it say?
- What does it say about God?
- What does that mean for me? How do I respond?

Use the team meetings as an opportunity to find out where the young people in your group are at spiritually – but be sensitive! You are likely to have a mixed group in which some people will never have heard the gospel and others will be committed Christians – this is both a challenge and an excellent opportunity for the young people to learn from you and each other.

You may want to start each team meeting with a short prayer and encourage the young people to be involved as the week progresses.

Session 5: Memory Verse:
'But you will receive power when the Holy Spirit comes on you' **(Acts 1:8).**

Session 1: Memory Verse:
'The heavens declare the glory of God; the skies proclaim the work of his hands. Day after day they pour forth speech; night after night they display knowledge' **(Ps. 19:1-2).**

Session 6: Memory Verse:
'Everyone who competes in the games goes into strict training. They do it to get a crown that will not last; but we do it to get a crown that will last forever' **(I Cor. 9:25).**

Session 2: Memory Verse:
'All Scripture is God-breathed and is useful for teaching, rebuking, correcting and training in righteousness, so that the man of God may be thoroughly equipped for every good work' **(2 Tim. 3:16-17).**

Session 7: Memory Verse:
'Your words are what sustains me; they are food for my hungry soul' **(Jer. 15:16).**

Session 3: Memory Verse:
'I am the way and the truth and the life. No one comes to the Father except through me' **(John 14:6).**

Session 4: Memory Verse:
'For the wages of sin is death, but the gift of God is eternal life in Christ Jesus our Lord' **(Rom. 6:23).**

Session 1: Challenge:
This week take 'time-out' to look up into the stars and ask yourself: What must this God be like to create such vast beauty? Next, ask yourself: Does the creator of the universe want to communicate with his creation – with me?

Session 2: Challenge:
If God designed you wouldn't He know best how you work? Get a good version of the Bible and start reading Mark from the New Testament.
Write down three ways God suggests you live and try to live them out this week.

Session 3: Challenge:
Do you know for certain that if you died today you would go to heaven? If you were standing before God and He said why should I let you in what would you say?

Session 4: Challenge:
Have you ever been given a gift? Well this week think about the most awesome gift you can ever and will ever receive. Eternal life from Jesus Christ. Happy Birthday and Merry Christmas all rolled into one – Big Time!

Session 5: Challenge:
Ask God to fill you with power. Ask God to fill you with his Spirit. Fire your old coach (self) and make Christ the centre of your life.

Session 6: Challenge:
Remember all that trust in Christ for salvation get a crown and an inheritance. It is like becoming a trillionaire and much more. We should be the happiest people on earth! It makes any other prize pale into insignificance!

Session 7: Challenge:
Just as I carve out time in my day to prepare for my sport, I will carve out time to get spiritually prepped; food for my hungry soul!
Today I will read:_____